Odd Minute Maths 5

Stanley Althans and Margery Dent

Basil Blackwell

Contents

page	**Number**
3	Products
4	Remainders
8	Thousands
10	Multiplying
13	Dividing
14	Sevens
23	Factors
26	More dividing

Fractions

5	Equivalent fractions
20	Fractional parts
25	Fractions on the clock

Measurement

2	Perimeters
6	Metres and centimetres
9	Kilograms and grams
17	Capacity
22	Length
27	Length in decimals

Shape and Geometry

7	Symmetry
11	Perpendicular and parallel
18	Measuring surfaces
24	Angles
28	Squares

page	**Money**
1	Shopping
21	Decimal money

Time

12	Years
19	Timetables

Revision

15	A check up
16	Still checking up
29	Do you remember?
30	A final check-up

Teacher's note
Each set is divided into three sections:

 simple problems are presented in practical situations

 the problems concentrate on the use of mathematical language

 mechanical examples provide reinforcement and practice

© 1985 S. Althans and M. Dent
All rights reserved
Published by Basil Blackwell Ltd, Oxford, England
ISBN 0 631 90730 0
Designed and typeset by DP Press Ltd, Sevenoaks, Kent
Printed by Thomson Litho Ltd, East Kilbride, Scotland

Shopping 1

1. Jill had £3.70 to spend, in 5 coins. What were they?
2. In the market she bought 2 jars of jam costing 48p each. How much did she pay?
3. She paid with a £1 coin. What was the change?
4. How much did she have left from her £3.70?
5. She then bought 4 oranges at 9p each, and a bunch of grapes for 56p. These cost ____ altogether.
6. She had spent £1.88 altogether. How much had she left?

 Find the cost of **one** in each case:
1. 5 doughnuts cost 45p
2. A dozen rolls cost 60p
3. 4 loaves cost £1.84
4. Half a dozen cream cakes cost £1.68
5. 8 buns cost £1.20

☾
1. £0.09 + £0.14 = ____
2. £1.23 + £0.46 = ____
3. £1.46 + £1.29 = ____
4. £1.75 + £2.53 = ____
5. £2.58 + £0.65 = ____
6. £1.67 + £2.33 = ____
7. £4.64 + £5.36 = ____

2 Perimeters

1. In a park, a rectangular sandpit is 3 m long and 2 m wide. What is the perimeter?
2. The paddling pool is square, 16 m all round. How long is each side?
3. The restaurant is pentagon shaped (5 sides). Each side is 4 m long. What is the perimeter of the restaurant?
4. The triangular sections of the roof each have two equal sides, 5 m long. The perimeter of each section is ____ m.
5. Hexagonal paving stones surround the restaurant. Find their perimeter, when each side is 25 cm long.
6. Two of these paving stones fitted together have a perimeter of ____ m ____ cm.

 Find the length of the unmarked sides.

1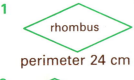
rhombus
perimeter 24 cm

3
parallelogram
perimeter 26 cm

5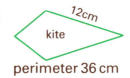
kite
perimeter 36 cm

2
regular octagon
perimeter 32 cm

4
star
perimeter 1 metre

1 $8 \times 7 =$ ____
2 $9 \times 6 =$ ____
3 $4 \times 8 =$ ____
4 $5 \times 7 =$ ____
5 $2 \times 9 =$ ____
6 $8 \times 8 =$ ____
7 $7 \times 7 =$ ____

Products 3

1. Farmer Brown added 8 rows, 7 in a row, to his orchard of plum trees. How many more trees did he plant?
2. He already had 6 rows of 7 trees each. How many trees did he have altogether?
3. He planned to have 112 trees. How many rows did this make?
4. He will pick 20 kg of plums from each tree. What weight will he get from 112 trees?
5. He packed his lettuces in a box, 6 along and 5 across. How many were in each layer?
6. He packed 5 dozen lettuces in each box. How many layers were there?
7. He sold each lettuce for 10p, so he got £_____ for every 60.

1. What is 5 times 9?
2. Multiply 8 by 12.
3. Find the product of 9 and 8.
4. Multiply 6 by itself.
5. Double 12, and double the answer.

1. $6 \times 7 =$ _____
2. $8 \times 9 =$ _____
3. $10 \times 10 =$ _____
4. $12 \times 6 =$ _____
5. $15 \times 5 =$ _____
6. $18 \times 6 =$ _____
7. $14 \times 5 =$ _____

4 Remainders

1 The 26 children in Class 3 were going on a trip. With 6 cars, 4 to a car, how many children would be left behind?
2 If there were 7 cars, how many empty places would there be?
3 With 7 cars and only 3 to a car, how many would remain behind?
4 But with 8 cars and 3 to a car, there would still be ____ left behind.
5 They could use two 15-seater minibuses, but this would leave ____ empty seats.
6 They could divide themselves equally between the two buses but there would still be ____ empty seats in each.

1 What number, divided by 4, gives 7 with 2 left over?
2 An **odd** number divided by 2 has ____ for the remainder.
3 Bob divided a number by 5. He gave an answer '6 rem 5'. What was the right answer?
4 The remainder is 3. What is the smallest number we could have divided by?
5 What is the greatest number left over when dividing by 7?

1 14 ÷ 3 = ____ r ____
2 20 ÷ 8 = ____ r ____
3 37 ÷ 6 = ____ r ____
4 39 ÷ 4 = ____ r ____
5 87 ÷ 10 = ____ r ____
6 78 ÷ 9 = ____ r ____
7 52 ÷ 5 = ____ r ____

Equivalent fractions 5

 A piece of string is 24 cm long.

1. 1 cm is $\frac{\square}{24}$ of the whole piece
2. 2 cm is $\frac{\square}{24}$ of the whole piece → $\frac{1}{\square}$
3. 8 cm is $\frac{\square}{24}$ of the whole piece → $\frac{1}{\square}$
4. 12 cm is $\frac{\square}{24}$ of the whole piece → $\frac{1}{\square}$
5. 6 cm is $\frac{\square}{24}$ of the whole piece → $\frac{1}{\square}$
6. 3 cm is $\frac{\square}{24}$ of the whole piece → $\frac{1}{\square}$
7. 4 cm is $\frac{\square}{24}$ of the whole piece → $\frac{1}{\square}$

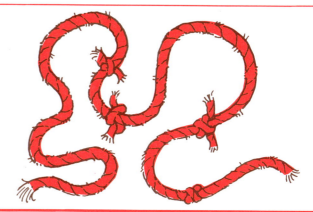

| starlings | robins | sparrows | blue tits | magpies |

Brian recorded the birds he had seen.
What fraction were:

1. magpies → $\frac{\square}{12}$
2. robins → $\frac{\square}{12} = \frac{1}{\square}$
3. blue tits → $\frac{\square}{12} = \frac{1}{\square}$
4. starlings → $\frac{\square}{12} = \frac{1}{\square}$
5. sparrows → $\frac{\square}{12} = \frac{1}{\square}$

1. $\frac{5}{10} = \frac{1}{\square}$
2. $\frac{2}{16} = \frac{1}{\square}$
3. $\frac{\square}{10} = \frac{1}{5}$
4. $\frac{\square}{4} = \frac{1}{2}$
5. $\frac{\square}{8} = \frac{1}{4}$
6. $\frac{3}{9} = \frac{1}{\square}$
7. $\frac{\square}{24} = \frac{1}{6}$

6 Metres and centimetres

Linda is 1 m 20 cm tall. Her desk is 59 cm high.
1. How much taller is Linda than her desk?
2. Her chair is 42 cm high.
   How much lower is the chair than Linda?
3. Linda's baby sister is half as tall as Linda.
   How tall is the baby?
4. Linda's mother is 27 cm taller than Linda.
   How tall is she?
5. Linda's father is half as tall again as Linda.
   How tall is he?
6. In a photograph she appears only one-sixth of her size.
   How tall is she in the picture?

How many **centimetres** in:
1. one-tenth of a metre?
2. one-fifth of a metre?
3. half of 3 metres?
4. a quarter of 8 metres?
5. a third of $1\frac{1}{2}$ metres?

1. 80 cm + 20 cm = _____ m
2. 2 m 70 cm + 30 cm = _____ m
3. 4 m 20 cm − 70 cm = _____ m _____ cm
4. 3 m 10 cm − 80 cm = _____ m _____ cm
5. 6 m × 5 = _____ m
6. 4 m 50 cm × 4 = _____ m
7. 1 m 25 cm × 8 = _____ m

Symmetry 7

Draw each shape with its mirror image.

1

2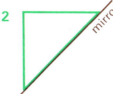

3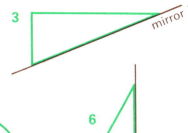

4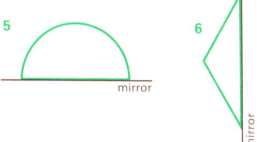

5, 7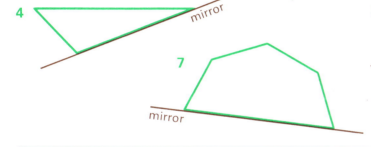

6

1 What capital letters of the alphabet between I and N have **mirror** (line) **symmetry**?

2 Name a line of symmetry of a circle.

3 A H N T   One of these letters has no line of symmetry. Which is it?

4 One letter in question 3 has **two** lines of symmetry. Which is it?

1 50 + 51 + 52 = ____
2 72 + 74 + 76 = ____
3 33 + 35 + 37 = ____
4 101 + 102 + 103 = ____
5 202 + 204 + 206 = ____
6 303 + 305 + 307 = ____
7 25 + 30 + 35 = ____

8 Thousands

The table shows the heights of five mountains.
1. Which is the highest?
2. Put the mountains in order of height, lowest first.
3. How much higher is the highest than the lowest?
4. Which two mountains are within 1000 m of each other in height?
5. What is the actual difference in the heights of these two?
6. About how many times higher is Everest than the Matterhorn?
7. About how many times higher is Everest than Snowdon?

Mountain	Height (metres)
Aconcagua	6950
Everest	8847
Kilimanjaro	5955
Matterhorn	4478
Snowdon	1080

1. How many hundreds are there in a thousand?
2. How many tens in a thousand?
3. What number is ten more than a thousand?
4. What number is ten less than a thousand?
5. How many is half of a thousand?

Write the **largest** number using:
1. 3, 6, 4, 7
2. 4, 2, 8, 1
3. 5, 0, 6, 2
4. 6, 8, 1, 4
5. 8, 4, 6, 5
6. 4, 7, 3, 9
7. 6, 0, 6, 1

Kilograms and grams

1. Twenty-eight 1p coins weigh almost 100 g. How many weigh 1 kilogram?
2. Two hundred 20p coins weigh just 1 kilogram. How many grams does one of them weigh?
3. One hundred £1 coins weigh nearly 1 kilogram. How many coins weigh 50 g?
4. Nine 10p coins weigh about 100 g. How many weigh $\frac{1}{2}$ kilogram?
5. How much are $\frac{1}{4}$ kilogram of 2p coins worth, if 14 weigh almost 100 g?
6. Nine 5p coins weigh about 50 g. How many weigh 1 kilogram?
7. Two 50p coins weigh 27 grams. £50 worth of these coins weigh _____ kg _____ g.

50 g   100 g   200 g   500 g   1 kg

Using these weights:
1. how would you weigh 300 g?
2. how would you weigh 1150 g?
3. what is the greatest weight you can weigh?
4. explain how you would weigh 950 g.
5. explain how you would weigh 1 kg 450 g.

1. $1000 \div 2 =$ _____
2. $1000 \div 4 =$ _____
3. $1000 \div 10 =$ _____
4. $1000 \div 5 =$ _____
5. $1000 \div 8 =$ _____
6. $1000 \div 100 =$ _____
7. $1000 \div 20 =$ _____

10 Multiplying

1. There are 250 four-wheeled cars in a car park. How many tyres are they using altogether?
2. How many tyres are there altogether if each car carries a spare tyre?
3. There are 36 motor-cycles in the car park. How many tyres do they have?
4. 250 cars average 3 people per car. How many do all the cars carry?
5. Parking charge for cars is 50p. What is the total amount paid?
6. The charge for a motor-cycle is 25p. How much do the motor-cyclists pay altogether?
7. The car parking spaces are in six rows of 45 spaces. How many cars can be parked?

1. Work out the product of 26 and 9.
2. What number, divided by 5, gives an answer of 15?
3. How many is 8 times 15?
4. 15 + 15 + 15 + 15 + 15 + 15 + 15 + 15 = ____
5. How many halves are there in 24?

1. 25 × 4 = ____
2. 25 × 6 = ____
3. 25 × 2 = ____
4. 25 × 3 = ____
5. 25 × 5 = ____
6. 25 × 9 = ____
7. 25 × 8 = ____

Perpendicular and parallel 11

 Copy these letters.
Mark them with arrows ———→ for **parallel** lines.
Mark pairs of **perpendicular** lines like this: ⌐

1 T   2 M   3 Z   4 A

5 H   6 Y   7 K

 Complete these sentences:
1 Perpendicular lines make a **r** ____ **a** ____.
2 Lines drawn on either side of a ruler are ____.
3 Railway lines have to be ____.
4 Walls of a room are usually ____ to the floor.
5 At 9 o'clock the hands of a clock are ____.

1 20 ÷ 6 = ____ r ____
2 31 ÷ 9 = ____ r ____
3 56 ÷ 8 = ____ r ____
4 47 ÷ 5 = ____ r ____
5 25 ÷ 3 = ____ r ____
6 73 ÷ 10 = ____ r ____
7 42 ÷ 4 = ____ r ____

12   Years

How long did these people live?
1. Alfred the Great   848 to 899
2. William the Conqueror   1028 to 1087
3. Queen Elizabeth I   1533 to 1603
4. Oliver Cromwell   1599 to 1658
5. George Washington   1732 to 1799
6. Franklin D. Roosevelt   1882 to 1945
7. Julius Caesar   100 BC to 44 BC

1. How many days make a **leap** year?
2. How many years in a century?
3. George Washington lived in the ____th century.
4. How many weeks in a year?
5. How many months in a quarter of a year?

1. 1000 − 150 = ____
2. 1215 − 1106 = ____
3. 1415 − 713 = ____
4. 1314 − 327 = ____
5. 1625 − 128 = ____
6. 1492 − 565 = ____
7. 1588 − 1397 = ____

Dividing   13

  These were the prices for holidays in Spain.
Work out the daily cost.

1. A week for £217
2. 8 days for £232
3. 9 days for £243
4. 10 days for £255
5. The 10-day holiday offered half price for children aged 5 to 12. How much was this for one child?
6. The 10-day holiday offered $\frac{1}{3}$ price for children under 5. How much was this?
7. An extra week cost only £35. How much was this per day?

1. What number is 17 multiplied by to get 170?
2. How many sixes in 42?
3. How many 8s can be taken from 72?
4. What is $\frac{1}{5}$ of 60?
5. How many groups of 7 make 28?

1. $64 \div 8 =$ _____
2. $25 \div 5 =$ _____
3. $16 \div 4 =$ _____
4. $100 \div 10 =$ _____
5. $36 \div 6 =$ _____
6. $81 \div 9 =$ _____
7. $9 \div 3 =$ _____

14   Sevens

1. How many days are there in five weeks?
2. How many weeks has February 1987?
3. How many whole weeks has June, and how many days left over?
4. From 11th March to 1st April there are ____ weeks.
5. Find the total number of days in the **31 day** months.
6. 1988 has ____ weeks and ____ days extra.
7. What is the next date in May in this sequence: 1st, 8th, 15th, 22nd, ____?

1. What number is **7 multiplied by itself**?
2. How many is seven dozen?
3. $7 \times 23 = 161 \rightarrow 7 \times 24 =$ ____
4. How many quarters are there in 7 whole ones?
5. What is the product of 7 and 8?

1. ____ $\div 6 = 7$
2. $7 \times 7 \times 7 =$ ____
3. $7 + 7 + 7 =$ ____
4. $0 \times 7 \times 7 =$ ____
5. $1421 \div 7 =$ ____
6. $(4 \times 7) + (6 \times 7) =$ ____
7. $77 \times 7 =$ ____

A check-up

1. Sue spent £1.35.
   How much change did she have from £2?
2. Each row of a pegboard has 8 holes.
   There are 160 holes altogether.
   How many rows are there?
3. A 90 cm length of cord is divided into eleven
   8 cm lengths. How much is left over?
4. Jane is 9 years old. Her father is 36.
   What fraction is Jane's age of her father's age?
   Write this in its simplest form.
5. Moving from the 12 to 4 the tip of the minute hand
   travels 35 cm. In 1 hour the tip moves ____ m ____ cm.
6. Which of these letters has line symmetry? R S T
7. Write the largest number made from these digits: 5, 2, 7, 4

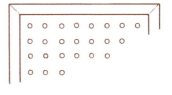

1. How many pence is £0.05?
2. What fraction of a kilogram is 250 g?
3. How many thirds in 9?
4. Which is the next leap year after 1990?
5. What fraction of the diameter of a circle is the radius?

1. £0.80 + £0.75 = ____
2. 19 × 8 = ____
3. 76 ÷ 4 = ____
4. 83 ÷ 9 = ____
5. $\frac{1}{3} = \frac{\Box}{12}$
6. $\frac{4}{16} = \frac{1}{\Box}$
7. 1000 − 12 = ____

16 Still checking up

1. Look at the corner of the hexagonal prism. How many right-angles are there?
2. How many pairs of parallel edges have the **hexagonal** faces?
3. How many months are there in $\frac{1}{6}$ of a year?
4. A soldier marched 8 metres in ten even paces. How long was each stride?
5. Which coin does not fit in this set?
   1p, 2p, 5p, 10p, 20p
6. A kite is folded about its line of symmetry. What shape is formed?
7. In a collection of marbles weighing 102 g, each one weighs 6 g. How many are there?

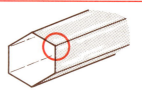

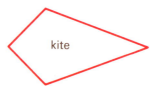
kite

1. Write **1001** in words.
2. Make £1.47 using five coins.
3. How many sweets do 7 children share when they have 12 each?
4. How many hours in a week?
5. What fraction of a day is 8 hours?

1. $23 + 17 - 19 = $ _____
2. $0 \times 1 \times 2 \times 3 = $ _____
3. $57 \div 8 = $ _____
4. $3 \times 3 \times 3 \times 3 = $ _____
5. $3 + 3 + 3 + 3 = $ _____
6. $740 \div 10 = $ _____
7. $8 \times 108 = $ _____

Capacity

1. A chemist has 14 half-litre bottles of medicine. How many litres is this?
2. From one $\frac{1}{2}$-litre bottle, he pours 110 ml. How much is left?
3. He uses a half of another half-litre bottle? How many millilitres are left in this bottle?
4. To make up a medicine he uses 25 ml from one bottle and 50 ml from each of two others. How much does he use?
5. What fraction of a litre does he use for this medicine?
6. He writes on the bottle: 'Take 5 ml, 3 times a day for a week'. How much will be taken altogether?
7. How many millilitres should be left out of 125 ml in the bottle?

1. How many millilitres are there in $\frac{1}{2}$ litre?
2. How many millilitres in $\frac{1}{4}$ litre?
3. What fraction of a litre is 100 ml?
4. What fraction of a litre is 200 ml?
5. What fraction of a litre is 1 ml?

1. $\frac{1}{10}$ of 1000 = _____
2. $\frac{1}{5}$ of 1000 = _____
3. $\frac{1}{4}$ of 1000 = _____
4. $\frac{1}{8}$ of 1000 = _____
5. $\frac{1}{100}$ of 1000 = _____
6. $\frac{1}{50}$ of 1000 = _____
7. $\frac{1}{25}$ of 1000 = _____

18 Measuring surfaces

Look at the picture of the **Manster**.
1. How many square units does the hair cover?
2. How many square units does the face cover?
3. How many square units does his body cover?
4. How many square units does the **Manster** cover altogether?
5. How many square units is the picture altogether?
6. How many square units are not covered by the **Manster**?
7. Find the difference in the space occupied by the **Manster** and the rest of the space.

 1 square unit

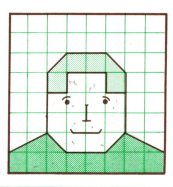

What is the length of the side of a square that covers:
1. 16 square units?
2. 36 square units?
3. 9 square units?
4. 49 square units?
5. 25 square units?

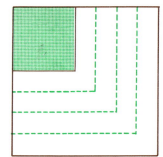

1. 25 × 6 = _____
2. 34 × 8 = _____
3. 46 × 7 = _____
4. 37 × 9 = _____
5. 63 × 4 = _____
6. 55 × 8 = _____
7. 73 × 3 = _____

Timetables 19

 This is the timetable for the morning trains between Witley and Playford.

1. How frequently do the trains run?
2. How long is the journey from Witley to Playford?
3. How long does the journey from Ringdon to Finston take?
4. When should the second train arrive at Playford?
5. At what time should the third train arrive at Finston?
6. How long is it between the first and the last morning trains?

Witley	7.30	8.50	10.10	11.30
Ringdon	7.55	9.15	10.35	11.55
Finston	8.20	9.40		12.20
Playford	9.05		11.45	

 This notice is outside a doctor's surgery.

1. How long is Dr F at the surgery each week?
2. How long is Dr M at the surgery each week?
3. How long is Dr K at the surgery each week?
4. Who spends most time at the surgery?
5. On which days is there no afternoon surgery?

```
        Surgery Hours
Mon   9.00 – 10.00 a.m.   Dr F
      5.00 –  6.30 p.m.   Dr M
Tues  9.00 – 10.00 a.m.   Dr M
      2.15 –  3.00 p.m.   Dr K
Wed   9.00 – 10.30 a.m.   Dr F
      5.00 –  6.30 p.m.   Dr F
Thurs 9.00 – 10.30 a.m.   Dr K
Fri   9.00 – 10.30 a.m.   Dr F
      5.00 –  6.30 p.m.   Dr F
Sat   9.00 – 10.00 a.m.   Dr K
```

1. 214 − 72 = _____
2. 343 − 127 = _____
3. 504 − 256 = _____
4. 625 − 369 = _____
5. 441 − 225 = _____
6. 576 − 329 = _____
7. 800 − 207 = _____

20   Fractional parts

1. How many unit squares make up the large square?
2. What fraction of the whole is 1 unit square?
3. The vertically shaded area is $\frac{1}{\Box}$ of the whole.
4. The horizontally shaded area is $\frac{1}{\Box}$ of the whole.
5. The sloping shaded area is $\frac{1}{\Box}$ of the whole.
6. How many unit squares make one-quarter of the whole?
7. How many unit squares are a half of the whole?

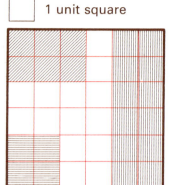

1 unit square

The hand of a clock starts at 12.
Which number will it point to after:

1. $\frac{1}{2}$ turn?
2. $\frac{1}{4}$ turn?
3. $\frac{1}{3}$ turn?
4. $\frac{1}{12}$ turn?
5. $\frac{1}{6}$ turn?

1. $\frac{1}{2}$ of $(8 + 14) =$ _____
2. $\frac{1}{4}$ of $(15 + 13) =$ _____
3. $\frac{1}{4}$ of $36 - \frac{1}{2}$ of $14 =$ _____
4. $\frac{1}{4}$ of $28 + \frac{1}{3}$ of $15 =$ _____
5. $\frac{1}{3}$ of $18 + \frac{1}{6}$ of $24 =$ _____
6. $\frac{1}{3}$ of $(31 - 4) =$ _____
7. $\frac{1}{5}$ of $35 - \frac{1}{3}$ of $9 =$ _____

Decimal money   21

  Use the **price list** to work out the cost of:
1. a lamp and a battery
2. a pair of mudguards
3. four batteries
4. a tyre and a wheel
5. a lamp and a bell
6. a mudguard and a tyre
7. How much more does a wheel cost than the mudguard and tyre together?

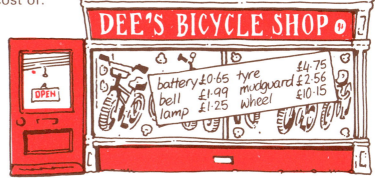

battery £0.65   tyre £4.75
bell £1.99   mudguard £2.56
lamp £1.25   wheel £10.15

1. How many pence are there in £0.45?
2. Write 12p as pounds.
3. How many 18 pence are there in £1.80?
4. Divide £2.60 by 10.
5. Find the value of fifty 5p coins.

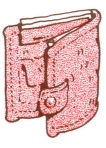

1. £0.65 + £0.35 = _____
2. £0.76 + £1.24 = _____
3. £3.27 + £2.38 = _____
4. £9.06 + £0.95 = _____
5. £6.08 − £0.45 = _____
6. £7.15 − £2.27 = _____
7. £10.00 − £1.25 = _____

22 Length

1. If each edge of a 20p coin is 9 mm long, its perimeter is ____ cm ____ mm.
2. If each edge of a 50p coin is 13 mm long, this is ____ cm ____ mm all round.
3. The perimeter of a 50p coin is ____ cm ____ mm.
4. The 20p coin rolls round ten times. It has rolled ____ cm.
5. The 50p coin rolls round ten times. It has rolled ____ cm.
6. The 20p coin has rolled ____ cm short of a metre.
7. The 50p coin has rolled ____ cm short of a metre.

1. How many **centimetres** make a metre?
2. How many **millimetres** make a centimetre?
3. How many **millimetres** make a metre?
4. Which is longest: 234 mm or $\frac{1}{4}$ m or 24 cm?
5. Put these in order, shortest first:
   205 mm, $\frac{1}{5}$ m, 25 cm

1. 6 cm = ____ mm
2. 15 cm = ____ mm
3. 70 mm = ____ cm
4. 210 mm = ____ cm
5. 5 m = ____ cm
6. 700 cm = ____ m
7. 8 m = ____ mm

Factors

  1 Six soldiers can parade in equal lines: in 1 line of 6, 6 lines of 1, 2 lines of 3, 3 lines of 2. That is in ____ ways.
2 How many ways can 8 soldiers parade in equal lines: 1 line of 8, 8 lines of 1, ____ lines of ____, ____ lines of ____. That is in ____ ways.
3 Arrange 9 soldiers in equal lines in as many ways as possible.
4 Ten soldiers can be arranged in ____ ways in equal lines.
5 In how many ways can 7 soldiers be arranged in equal lines?
6 In how many ways can 15 soldiers be arranged in equal lines?
7 Arrange 16 soldiers in equal lines in as many ways as possible.

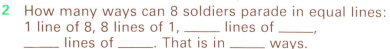
2 lines of 3

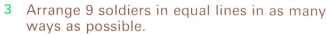
3 lines of 2

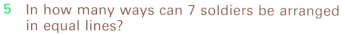
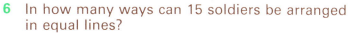
1 line of 6

6 lines of 1

  1 Complete the set of factors of 6: 1, ____, ____, 6.
2 Complete the set of factors of 12: 1, ____, ____, ____, ____, 12.
3 Write the set of factors of 8.
4 Write the set of factors of 25.
5 Write the set of factors of 24.

  1 $36 \div 4 =$ ____
2 $36 \div 9 =$ ____
3 $36 \div 3 =$ ____
4 $36 \div 6 =$ ____
5 $36 \div 1 =$ ____
6 $36 \div 2 =$ ____
7 $36 \div 36 =$ ____

24 Angles

 Copy the shapes. Mark all the 90° angles (right-angles) like this: ⌐

1

2

3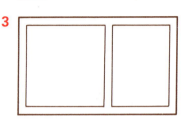

4

5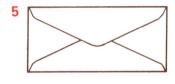

 From this set choose members that are:
1. right-angles
2. more than a right-angle
3. two right-angles
4. parallel
5. half a right-angle

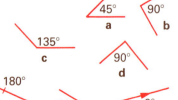

1. 90 ÷ 2 = _____
2. 90 ÷ 10 = _____
3. 90 ÷ 3 = _____
4. 90 ÷ 6 = _____
5. 90 × 2 = _____
6. 90 × 3 = _____
7. 90 × 4 = _____

Fractions on the clock 25

   1 What fraction of a whole turn does the hour hand of Big Ben make in 1 hour?
2 What fraction of a whole turn does the minute hand of Big Ben make in a minute?
3 The hour hand moves one-third of the way round: how many hours is this?
4 The minute hand moves one-third of the way round: how many minutes is this?
5 How many minutes in one-fifth of an hour?
6 What fraction of a whole turn does the minute hand move in ten minutes?
7 What fraction of a whole turn does the hour hand move in 30 minutes?

   What fraction of a turn has the **hour** hand made moving from:
1 Z → Y?
2 Z → X?
3 Z → W?
4 Y → X?
5 X → W?

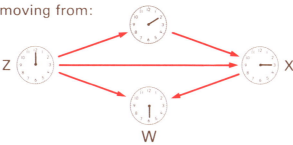

   1 $\frac{1}{4}$ of 60 = _____
2 $\frac{1}{3}$ of 60 = _____
3 $\frac{1}{2}$ of 60 = _____
4 $\frac{1}{10}$ of 60 = _____
5 $\frac{1}{6}$ of 60 = _____
6 $\frac{1}{5}$ of 60 = _____
7 $\frac{1}{20}$ of 60 = _____

26 More dividing

  On a TV screen:
1. A desk 60 cm tall appears $\frac{1}{10}$ of its true size.
   How high is it in the picture?
2. An elephant 2 m tall appears $\frac{1}{20}$ of its normal size.
   How tall is it on the picture?
3. A lady 1 m 50 cm tall appears $\frac{1}{30}$ of her true size.
   How tall is she in the picture?
4. A boy 1 m 20 cm tall appears 30 cm tall.
   What fraction of his height is the size of the picture?
5. A tree 4 m high appears 20 cm tall.
   What fraction is the size of the picture?
6. A building 30 m high appears 30 cm tall.
   What fraction is the size of the picture?
7. A close-up picture of a butterfly is 12 cm across.
   Its true width is 4 cm. How many times is it enlarged?

  A money-box contains 480 pennies.
How much would each get if they were shared among:
1. 20 children?
2. 30 children?
3. 40 children?
4. 60 children?
5. 80 children?

1. 260 ÷ 10 = ____
2. 320 ÷ 40 = ____
3. 540 ÷ 60 = ____
4. 810 ÷ 90 = ____
5. 720 ÷ 80 = ____
6. 630 ÷ 90 = ____
7. 490 ÷ 70 = ____

Length in decimals   27

 Measure these lines.
Write their lengths in mm and in cm, like this: 27 mm, 2.7 cm.

1 ─────────────
2 ──────────────────
3 ────────────────────
4 ──────────────
5 ────────────────────────
6 ──────────────────
7 ────────────────────

1 How many millimetres are there in 0.5 cm?
2 How many centimetres in 0.5 m?
3 How many millimetres in $\frac{1}{2}$ metre?
4 Which is longest, $\frac{1}{2}$ m or 55 cm or 505 mm?
5 Which is shortest, 4 mm or $\frac{1}{2}$ cm or 0.5 cm?

1 2.0 cm = _____ mm
2 1.5 cm = _____ mm
3 4.7 cm = _____ mm
4 0.6 cm = _____ mm
5 10 mm = _____ cm
6 24 mm = _____ cm
7 5 mm = _____ cm

28 Squares

1. Find the perimeter of a square with sides 6 cm long.
2. A square has a perimeter of 36 cm. How long is each side?
3. How many right-angles are there in this square?
4. How many lines of mirror symmetry has a square?
5. A square is folded on its lines of symmetry. What shapes are formed?
6. How many square faces has a cube?
7. How many pairs of parallel sides has a square?

Find the number of centimetre squares that fit on to these squares:
1. sides 5 cm long
2. sides 6 cm long
3. sides 7 cm long
4. sides 8 cm long
5. sides 9 cm long

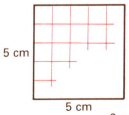
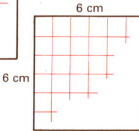

1. 7 × 7 = _____
2. 8 × 8 = _____
3. 9 × 9 = _____
4. 10 × 10 = _____
5. 11 × 11 = _____
6. 12 × 12 = _____
7. 13 × 13 = _____

29 Do you remember?

 1 A litre of petrol costs £0.42.
  How much do 5 litres cost?

2 The perimeter of an equilateral triangle is 27 cm.
  Find the length of each side.

3 259 daffodils are planted in 8 equal rows.
  How many are planted in each row?
  How many are left over?

4 The fraction of the hexagon shaded is $\frac{\Box}{6} = \frac{1}{\Box}$.

5 Twenty centimetres is cut from a piece of ribbon 1 m 10 cm long. How much is left?

6 Draw this shape, with its mirror image.
  What is the shape you have drawn?

7 Add 750 g and 250 g. Answer in kilograms.

 1 How many days are there in 7 weeks?
2 How many pence in £1.05?
3 How many centimetres in $\frac{1}{4}$ metre?
4 How many grams in a kilogram?
5 How many years in half a century?

 1 $7 \times 6 = $ _____
2 $8 \times 7 = $ _____
3 $7 \times 4 = $ _____
4 $9 \times 7 = $ _____
5 $7 \times 3 = $ _____
6 $0 \times 7 = $ _____
7 $5 \times 7 = $ _____

30　　　　　　　　　　　　　　　　　　A final check-up

1. How many millilitres are needed for a half-full litre-flask of water?
2. How many unit squares can be fitted on to the hexagon? The shaded area is 1 unit ^{2}.
3. I waited 8 minutes for a bus which came at 12.03 p.m. When did I reach the bus-stop?
4. Sally won a race in 1 min 58 seconds. Elise was 5 seconds slower. How long did she take?
5. Find the change from £3 after spending £2.45.
6. How many centimetres are there in 2.07 metres?
7. Which of this set are factors of 24?
   1, 2, 3, 4, 5, 6, 7, 8, 9

1. How many degrees are there in a right-angle?
2. What fraction of a turn does the hour hand make moving from 4 to 8?
3. Share 540 sweets equally between 60 children.
4. How many millimetres in a metre?
5. How many 200 ml-bottles can be filled from a litre?

1. $26 \times 8 =$ _____
2. $34 \times 5 =$ _____
3. $17 \times 6 =$ _____
4. $54 \times 3 =$ _____
5. $23 \times 9 =$ _____
6. $46 \times 7 =$ _____
7. $68 \times 4 =$ _____